A CONCATENATION

A
Concatenation

of words by a variety of hands
with wood engravings
of a variety of cats
by

Yvonne Skargon

PRIMROSE HILL PRESS

LONDON

First published by Primrose Hill Press 2000
ISBN 1 901 648 21 4

Engravings and selection © 2000 Yvonne Skargon
This edition © 2000 Primrose Hill Press

British Library Catalogue-in-Publication Data
A catalogue record of this book is available
from the British Library

Typeset by
Oblong Creative Ltd, Otley, West Yorkshire
and printed and bound in England by
Smith Settle Ltd, Otley, West Yorkshire

THE PLAIN FACTS
By a Plain but Amiable Cat

See what a charming smile I bring,
Which no one can resist;
For I have found a wondrous thing –
The fact that I exist.

And I have found another, which
I now proceed to tell.
The world is so sublimely rich
That you exist as well.

Fact One is lovely, so is Two,
But O the best is Three:
The Fact that I can smile at you,
And you can smile at me.

Ruth Pitter from *End of Drought*

A poet's cat, sedate and grave
As poet well could wish to have,
Was much addicted to inquire
For nooks to which she might retire,
And where, secure as mouse in chink,
She might repose, or sit and think.
I know not where she caught the trick –
   Nature perhaps herself had cast her
In such a mould philosophique,
   Or else she learned it of her master.
Sometimes ascending, debonair,
An apple tree, or lofty pear,
Lodged with convenience in the fork,
She watched the gardener at his work;
Sometimes her ease and solace sought
In an old empty watering pot;
There, wanting nothing save a fan,
To seem some nymph in her sedan
Apparelled in exactest sort,
And ready to be borne to court.

William Cowper *The Retired Cat*

My cat won't eat mice; he just doesn't fancy them. He will only catch one as a game.

When he has had enough of play he will spare its life and take himself off to other dreams.

He sits in the loop of his tail, all innocence, his head like a clenched fist.

But thanks to his claws, the mouse is dead.

I tell him 'Catch the mouse and leave the birds alone!'

But it is rather complicated, and sometimes even the nicest cat will get it wrong.

Jules Reynard from *Hunting with the Fox*

Life is to be fortified by many friendships. To love, and to be loved, is the greatest happiness of existence.

Sydney Smith in *Lady Holland, Memoir* 1855

It is bred and is an inhabitant of almost all countries in the world, all Cats were at first wild, but were at length tamed by the Industry of Mankind; it is a Beast of prey, even the tame one, more especially the wild, it being in the opinion of many nothing but a diminutive Lyon.

William Salmon *The English Physician, or the Druggist Shop Opened* 1693

Cat! who hast pass'd thy grand climacteric,
   How many mice and rats hast in thy days
   Destroy'd? – How many tit bits stolen? Gaze
With those bright languid segments green, and prick
Those velvet ears – but pr'ythee do not stick
   Thy latent talons in me – and upraise
   Thy gentle mew – and tell me all thy frays
Of fish and mice, and rats and tender chick.
   Nay, look not down, nor lick thy dainty wrists –
For all thy wheezy asthma, – and for all
   Thy tail's tip is nick'd off – and though the fists
Of many a maid have given thee many a maul,
   Still is that fur as soft as when the lists
In youth thou enter'dst on glass bottled wall.

John Keats *To Mrs Reynolds' Cat*

There is a propensity belonging to common house-cats that is very remarkable; I mean their violent fondness for fish, which appears to be their most favourite food: and yet nature in this instance seems to have planted in them an appetite that, unassisted, they know not how to gratify: for of all quadrupeds cats are the least disposed towards water; and will not, when they can avoid it, deign to wet a foot, much less to plunge into that element.

Gilbert White *The Natural History of Selbourne* 12 May 1770

Alison's novel *Foreign Affairs* is being considered for TV by Granada, it might be funny dramatized if well done. There is always the danger the best bits will be removed, or misinterpreted. V and I were very much amused by Alison saying she had been at what she regarded as grandish dinner party given by Diana Phipps, about sixteen people, where at the end of dinner Diana Phipps's cat jumped on the table, walked up and down as if owning the place, sampling remains of food, and being talked to by the guests. Alison said that in the US everyone would have had forty fits at such an incident. She could hardly believe – indeed refused to believe – we were speaking the truth in assuring her that no one here would think anything of it, indeed some people might say what an amusing, intelligent thing for the cat to do. They must persuade their cat to greet guests in that manner.

Anthony Powell *Journals* 23 May 1985

'You don't have to remember any of it, actually,' Jennie explained. 'All that you have to remember is Rule 1: "When in doubt – WASH!" '

From *Jennie* by Paul Gallico

The mice held a meeting to decide
How to protect themselves against the cat.
Some said this and some said that,
Till a young mouse spoke up boldly: 'I propose
That a bell should be tied
To the cat's neck so he can be heard
Coming round the corner, and we can hide.'
Unanimous applause. An old mouse rose
And remarked, 'That's all very well,
But who's going to attach the bell?'
Not one mouse volunteered a word.

Belling the Cat retold by James Michie from *Aesop's Fables*

All that matters is to be at one with the living God
to be a creature in the house of the God of Life.

Like a cat asleep on a chair
at peace, in peace
and at one with the master of the house, with the mistress,
at home, at home in the house of the living,
sleeping on the hearth, and yawning before the fire.

Sleeping on the hearth of the living world
yawning at home before the fire of life
feeling the presence of the living God
like a great reassurance
a deep calm in the heart
a presence
as of the master sitting at the board
in his own greater being,
in the house of life.

D. H. Lawrence *Pax*

It is snowing. Flakes are building up on the flowers and melting on the warm backs of beasts, leaving a sodden gloss. Max looks out in disgust before selecting the softest, warmest chair in the kitchen in which to winter. His green eyes close in prayer as he thanks God for creating men to wait on cats.

Ronald Blythe *Word from Wormingford*

… He is particularly fond of the spring garden … It is sheltered and secluded, and there are banks where he can lie in the sun, and cool retreats when it is too hot, and also Yews and Hollies, under which he can always find a dry place when other parts of the ground are damp. One bank is covered with Cerastium; this he thinks is just suitable for his bed. I often find him there, and though it is not quite the best thing for the Cerastium I cannot help admiring his beautiful rich tabby coat, with its large black clouds, so well set off by the velvety grey of the little downy plant. He is an old pussy now, and when you meet him coming along a path it must be confessed that he is too fat and has lost his figure. But it only shows when he is walking, for when he is sitting, or lying comfortably curled or tucked … you would never call him a fat old cat.

Gertrude Jekyll *Children and Gardens*

Musa then lifted her Eyes. The Time was Evening.
A Blackbird was setting his Rage at her Advent to Musick.
Small Moths swoopt by drunkenly, to be swip'd at;
In the Hedgerow the Shrew bustled by unsuspecting.
Behind her, in the bright Kitchen, she heard a Frying,
And after a moment's Reflexion, decided 'twas Haddock.
The Young in her Womb seem'd to lie easier.
Let her but get her Bellyful of Victuals,
And a small Sup of Cow's Milk for her innoxious Night-Draught,
Let her but chuse whose bed must carry double,
All would be well; she did not dread the Morning:
She dream'd of prowling through the rustling Coppice,
Of slinking between the Hedgerow and the Stubble
In dry, large-moon'd Octobers; of May-mornings
When the lush mowing-Grass should skreen her Hunting
And with soft Dew drench her white-velvet Bosom;
Of fishing-Expeditions in the Summer
And cozy Firesides and good Beds in Winter.
Her children should be hunters of the Mole, the stack-Rat
And of all Vermin; her Apotheosis
Was come upon her; she had been translated.

Ruth Pitter *Musa Translated* (with apologies to William Blake)

This beast is wonderful nimble, setting upon her prey like the Lyon, by leaping: and therefore she hunteth both Rats, all kinds of Myce, and Birds, eating not only them, but also Fish, wherewithall she is best pleased … It is needlesse to spend any time about her loving nature to man, how she flattereth by rubbing her skinne against one's Legges, how she whurleth with her voyce, having as many tunes as turnes, for she hath one voyce to beg and complain, another to testifie her delight and pleasure, another among her own kind by flattering, by hissing, by puffing, by spitting, insomuch as some have thought that they have a peculiar intelligible language among themselves. Therefore how she beggeth, playeth, leapeth, looketh, catcheth, tosseth with her foote, riseth up to strings held over her head, sometimes creeping, sometimes lying on the back, playing with one foot, sometimes on the bely, snatching, now with mouth, and anon with foot, apprehending greedily anything save the hand of a man with divers such gestical actions, it is needelesse to stand upon; insomuch as Cœlius was wont to say, that being free from his Studies and more urgent weighty affairs, he was not ashamed to play and sport himself with his cat, and verily it might well be called an idle man's pastime …

Edward Topsell *Historie of Foure-Footed Beastes* 1607

… One of these kittens was kept, who, as he was quite deaf, was unnamed, and became known by the servants as 'the master's cat', because of his devotion to my father. He was always with him, and used to follow him about the garden like a dog, and sit with him when he wrote. One evening we were all, except father, going to a ball, and when we started, left 'the master' and his cat in the drawing room together. 'The master' was reading at a small table; suddenly the candle went out. My father, who was much interested in his book, re-lighted the candle, stroked the cat, who was looking at him pathetically he noticed, and continued his reading. A few minutes later, as the light became dim, he looked up just in time to see puss deliberately put out the candle with his paw, and then look appealingly at him. This second and unmistakeable hint was not disregarded, and puss was given the petting he craved. Father was full of this anecdote when we all met at breakfast the next morning.

Mary Angela (Mamie) Dickens *My Father as I Recall Him* 1876

… I look like St. John, in the Isle of Patmos, writing revelations, and prophesying 'Woe! woe! woe! the Kingdom of desolation is at hand!' Indeed, I have prettier animals about me than he ever dreamt of; here is the dear Patapan, and a little Vandyke cat, with black whiskers and boots: you would swear it was of a very ancient family, in the west of England, famous for their loyalty …

Horace Walpole *to Lady Ossery* 14 July 1742

It is a feature of the artistic imagination that it should be able to reconstitute everything on the basis of very limited data. When Delacroix wanted to paint a tiger, he used his cat as a model.

Henry de Montherlant *The Goddess Cypris* 1944

There was another story in the paper a week or so since. A gentleman had a favourite cat whom he taught to sit at the dinner-table where it behaved very well. He was in the habit of putting any scraps he left on to the cat's plate. One day puss did not take his place punctually, but presently appeared with two mice, one of which it placed on its master's plate, the other on its own.

Beatrix Potter *Journal* 27 January 1884

I would put the drawbacks in town gardening in the follow-
ing order:– First, WALLS; second, AIR; third, CATS; fourth,
SOIL … Cats can almost break a gardener's heart.

Francis Eveleen, Lady Seton *My Town Garden* 1927

… as the learned and ingenious Montaigne says like himself freely, 'When my cat and I entertain each other with mutual apish tricks, as playing with a garter, who knows but that I make my cat more sport than she makes me? Shall I conclude her to be simple, that has her time to begin or refuse to play as freely as I myself have? Nay, who knows that it is a defect of my not understanding her language (for doubtless cats talk and reason with one another) that we agree no better? And who knows that she pities me for being no wiser than than to play with her, and laughs and censures my folly for making sport for her, when we two play together?'

Thus freely speaks Montaigne concerning cats …

Izaak Walton *Compleat Angler*

Why, Sir, a man grows better humoured as he grows older. He improves by experience. When young he thinks himself of great consequence and everything of importance. As he advances in life, he learns to think of himself as of no consequence and little things of little importance; and so he becomes more patient, and better pleased.

James Boswell *The Life of Samuel Johnson*

I still hope he may not come till I myself am home first! But – if he should – there is one thing you must attend to, and which you would not think of without being told! – that cat!! – I wish she were dead! But I can't shorten her days! because – you see – my poor dear wee dog liked her! Well! there she is – and as long as she attends Mr. C. at his meals (she doesn't care a snuff of tobacco for him at any other times!) so long will Mr. C. continue to give her bits of meat, and dribbles of milk, to the ruination of carpets and hearth rugs! – I have over and over again pointed out to him the stains she has made – but he won't believe them her doing! – And the dining room carpet was so old and ugly, that it wasn't worth rows with one's Husband about! Now, however, that nice new cloth must be protected against the Cat-abuse. So what I wish is that you would shut up the creature when Mr. C. has breakfast, or dinner, or tea. And if he remarks on her absence, say it was my express desire. He has no idea what a selfish, immoral, improper beast she is, nor what mischief she does to the carpets.

Jane Welsh Carlisle *to her housemaid, Jessie* 19 August 1865

The cat is domestic only as far as suits its own ends; it will not be kennelled or harnessed nor suffer any dictation as to its goings out or comings in. Long contact with the human race has developed in it the art of diplomacy, and no Roman Cardinal of mediæval days knew better how to ingratiate himself with his surroundings than a cat with a saucer of cream on its mental horizon. But the social smoothness, the purring innocence, the softness of the velvet paw may be laid aside at a moment's notice, and the sinuous feline may disappear, in deliberate aloofness, to a world of roofs and chimney-stacks, where the human element is distanced and disregarded.

Hector Hugh Munro ('Saki') *The Square Egg*

Stately, kindly, lordly friend
              Condescend
Here to sit by me, and turn
Glorious eyes that smile and burn,
Golden eyes, love's lustrous meed,
On the golden page I read.

All your wondrous wealth of hair
              Dark and fair,
Silken-shaggy, soft and bright
As the clouds and beams of night,
Pays my reverent hand's caress
Back with friendlier gentleness.

Dogs may fawn on all and some
              As they come;
You, a friend of loftier mind,
Answer friends alone in kind.
Just your foot upon my hand
Softly bids it understand.

Algernon Charles Swinburne *To a Cat*

… On that night when I went to bed about twelve o'clock I missed Toss, who is generally by the fire in the room where we sit; when I went upstairs there she was sitting upright in the middle of my bed waiting for me. There was no fire in the room, and she never sleeps on our bed, but that night she missed Flu, and came there to inquire for her and to keep me company. She curled herself up on the counterpane by my side, and whenever I woke up in the night she sat up instantly and looked at me; directly I lay down she curled herself up and slept again, and so she remained till I went down to breakfast the next morning. She is a most interesting cat, and we get fonder and fonder of her though we have just put her on two meals of meat a day instead of three, as we thought too much meat tended to promote inflammatory action of her lungs, which are delicate …

... I have just been called to the door by the sweet voice of Toss, whose morning proceedings are wonderful. She sleeps – she has just jumped on my lap, and her beautiful tail has made this smudge, but I have put her down again. I was going to say that she sleeps on an armchair before the drawing-room fire; descends the moment she hears the servants about in the morning and makes them let her out; comes back and enters Flu's room with Eliza regularly at half-past seven. Then she comes to my door and gives a mew, and then, especially if I let her in and go on writing or reading without taking any notice of her, there is a real demonstration of affection for five minutes such as never occurs again in the day. She purrs, she walks round and round me, she jumps in my lap, she turns to me and rubs her head and nose against my chin; she opens her mouth and raps her pretty white teeth against my pen; then she will jump down, settle herself down by the fire, and never show any more affection all day ...

Matthew Arnold *to his Mother* 21 February 1870 and 28 November 1871

Can you explain how and why cats make love to us? Tiber will come, if I am reading or writing or lying on my bed and will 'tease tow' with his claws. Then, coming closer, will gaze into my face, suddenly dig his pointed muzzle under my chin once or twice, retreat, roll on his side, inviting my hand, turn his head dreamily to one side, passive and luxurious. Then he will turn on me almost fiercely with a burst of purring, and so on, and so on.

But is this, as I think, reserved for human lovers? With a female cat I think he displays no such graces but is fiercely practical. It is more like the love that was shown him by his mother when he was a kitten. And naturally it is shown most strongly before and after I have fed him. But the luxury of his furry love is very beautiful.

David Garnett *to Sylvia Townsend Warner* 13 June 1973

… Tiber makes love to you for the good reason that he loves you, and loves making love. Cats are passionate and voluptuous, they get satisfaction from mating but no pleasure (the females dislike it, and this is wounding to the male), no voluptuousness; *and no appreciation.* Tiber has the pleasure of being pleased and knowing he pleases in his love-making with you. I am so glad you have each other. Does he roll on his head? Docs he fall asleep with an ownerly paw laid over you?

We had a dark grey cat (Norfolk bred, very Norfolk in character) called Tom. He was reserved, domineering, voluptuous – much as I imagine Tiber to be. When he was middle-aged he gave up nocturnal prowlings and slept on my bed, against my feet. One evening I was reading in bed when I became aware that Tom was staring at me. I put down my book, said nothing, watched. Slowly, with a look of intense concentration, he got up and advanced on me, like Tarquin with ravishing strides, poised himself, put out a front paw, and stroked my cheek as I used to stroke his chops. A human caress from a cat. I felt very meagre and ill-educated that I could not purr.

Sylvia Townsend Warner *to David Garnett* 18 June 1973

If a man does not make new acquaintance as he advances through life, he will soon find himself left alone. A man, Sir, should keep his friendship in *constant repair*.

James Boswell *The Life of Samuel Johnson*

Lovers and scholars, the ardent and the prim,
As they grow older, ripen; and love cats,
Those gentle household gods, those powerful pets,
Afraid of draughts, and sedentary, like them.

If only one could break their pride, how well
These voluptuary lovers of the dark
Who seek out silent corners where fears lurk
Would serve to draw the chariots of Hell.

Look at them dreaming: how that attitude
Suggests the Sphinx, which also dreams, and lies
Stretched out upon the sands of solitude.

Their fecund loins house magic powers; and see!
Like grains of sand that glint elusively,
The specks of gold inhabiting their eyes.

Charles Baudelaire *Cats* translated by Laurence Lerner

Puss grew presently familiar, would leap into my lap, raise himself upon his hinder feet, and bite the hair from my temples. He would suffer me to take him up, and to carry him about in my arms ... I made it my custom to carry him always after breakfast into the garden, where he hid himself generally under the leaves of a cucumber vine, sleeping or chewing the cud till evening; in the leaves also of that vine he found a favourite repast. I had not long habituated him to this taste of liberty, before he began to be impatient for the return of the time when he might enjoy it. He would invite me to the garden by drumming upon my knee, and by a look of such expression as it was not possible to misinterpret. If this rhetoric did not immediately succeed, he would take the skirt of my coat between his teeth, and pull it with all his force. Thus Puss might be said to be perfectly tamed; the shyness of his nature was done away, and on the whole it was visible by many symptoms, which I have not room to enumerate, that he was happier in human society than when shut up with his natural companions.

William Cowper *The Gentleman's Magazine* June 1784

I was induced, by various considerations, to institute some experiments, with a view to ascertaining what effects could be produced on brute creatures, by the agency of what has been called … animal magnetism …

My first experiments on animals were made on … four cats and kittens, at intervals, from the 16th May to the 3rd October, 1838, and each of them was put to sleep at the first trial; and ultimately, I was able to put first one and then another to sleep, and at the end to leave three sleeping together … One of these, a Tom, the first of them that was magnetised, became easily and strongly influenced … so that he has been pulled about, lifted up by the nape of the neck, and the ears tickled with a pen, during which he would remain motionless, and the

cat was then said to be in a state of catalepsy; sometimes when lifted up by the head or tail, the eyes might partially open without the limbs moving, and when dropped down, the eyes again closed, and he continued to sleep, without making any effort to move from the place where he had been dropped.

Dr. John Wilson (Physician to the Middlesex Hospital)
Trials of Animal Magnetism on the Brute Creation 1839

But first, in August, I went to London. Katherine needed warmer clothes for the coming winter, and Wingly was to be collected from the vet in London.

I stayed there about a week before I returned with Wingly. He travelled all the way in a collar and lead, like a dog. He was a beautiful, lordly, black-and-white cat and when the train stopped, as it frequently did, he and I walked up and down the platform to the astonishment and admiration of the French countryfolk. But, somehow, I never could persuade him that the tarred platforms were made of grass, with the necessary soil for him to scratch with fine soft paws. I began to despair, till on one very long platform we found a little grassy garden – and all was well.

Eventually we arrived safely at the chalet in Montana, and Wingly settled in, rather as a king might graciously accept a country house as the best his subjects could do. Presently, when the snow set in, he would sit at Katherine's window with his head going up and down like a mandarin watching these strange large white things falling, falling, but never going up again. It was freezing hard and Wingly soon learnt that the heavy curtain over the bathroom window was movable, and he would go out, coming back later with the snow on his coat frozen into tinkling drops of ice. Every evening, at ten o'clock, he would sit and lick his coat till it shone, then his ears and soft white paws. Katherine said that then he picked up his top hat, fixed a buttonhole in his fur and went out for his nightly stroll.

Ida Constance Baker *Katherine Mansfield – Memories of L. M.*

If the newspapers foretold a thaw my mother would shrug her shoulders and laugh scornfully. 'A thaw? Those Paris meteorologists can't teach me anything about that! Look at the cat's paws!' Feeling chilly, the cat had indeed folded her paws out of sight beneath her, and shut her eyes tight. 'When there's only going to be a short spell of cold,' went on Sido, 'the cat rolls herself into a turban with her nose against the root of her tail. But when it's going to be really bitter, she tucks in the pads of her front paws and rolls them up like a muff.'

Colette from *My Mother's House*

15 Clifford's Inn, E.C.

… No, I will not have any Persian cat; it is undertaking too much responsibility. I must have a cat whom I find homeless, wandering about the court, and to whom, therefore, I am under no obligation. There is a Clifford's Inn euphemism about cats which the laundresses use quite gravely: they say people come to this place 'to lose their cats'. They mean that, when they have a cat they don't want to kill and don't know how to get rid of, they bring it here, drop it inside the railings of our grass-plot, and go away under the impression that they have been 'losing' their cat. Well, this happens very frequently and I have already selected a dirty little drunken wretch of a kitten to be successor to my poor old cat. I don't suppose it drinks anything stronger than milk and water but then, you know, so much milk and water must be bad for a kitten that age – at any rate it looks as if it drank; but it gives me the impression of being affectionate, intelligent, and fond of mice, and I believe, if it had a home, it would become more respectable; at any rate I will see how it works.

Samuel Butler *to Miss Savage* 21 October 1885

Double, double, toil and trouble,
Crumps and bumps and lumps of rubble.
Little Mister, six weeks old,
Hungry, frightened, dirty, cold,
Has no mother, home, nor dinner,
But he's sharp for a beginner.
From his crevice he surveys
Those who walk the ruined ways;
From their faces he can tell
Who would treat a kitten well.
The big policeman, good but gruff –
Let him pass; he's rather rough,
And as a conscientious man
Might pop him in a certain Van.
A kindly matron comes to view.
She's nice – but what about the stew?
When her four fat kids have done
There's not much left for anyone.
Besides, those kids would give him hell.
Let her go, then. Wait a spell.
Here's a warden; that's a frost –
He's got no home except his post.
Soldier, sailor – damn, no good.
Cripes, he could down a bit of food.
And O hell, here comes the rain.
Stick it, Mister, try again.

Ah, here she comes, the very one!
The fact is obvious as the sun.
Young as he is, now Mister knows
He can bid farewell to woes.
In her countenance he reads
That she will satisfy his needs.

Food, fire, bed – he ticks them off –
Worm-dose, mixture for his cough,
Velvet mouse for when he plays,
Brush and comb, and holidays
In the countryside afar,
Or boarded out with loving char.
She will pick him up correctly
And always touch him circumspectly,
Like a really first-class mother
Never neglect, yet never bother.
The greatest wonder is that he
Knows that there is a vacancy,
Which has allowed a thieving band
Of mice to get the upper hand.

Forth he darts – with piteous grace
Looks up mewing in her face.
Six weeks old – but what a grip
On the art of salesmanship!
Youth, dirt, fear, all play their part
In the lady's feeling heart.
A word of love, a mutual kiss
And he is hers, and she is his.
Because he is so small and weak
She holds him closely to her cheek,
Takes him home, through wind and rain,
And will not let him go again.

Arrived, he finds he did not err
In his estimate of her.
Warm milk, a nice old woollen vest,
And he soon sinks to blissful rest.
When he awakes, his coat will be
Brushed into strict propriety,
And in the evening she will seal
Their love with a substantial meal,
And let him lay his clever head
Close to her own warm heart, in bed.

Ruth Pitter *Mister the Blitzkit*

Every visitor to Hanover Terrace will remember Caruso; he figured at meals on a chair beside Gosse, and was always to be found in his vicinity when he was reading or at work in his library. Like Bayle's friend, Mlle. Dupuy, who attributed her skill in playing the harp to the 'critical taste' of her favourite cat, Gosse seemed to draw some opiate quality for his nerves from the very proximity of Caruso, and his predecessors and successors. The serenity and majestic indifference, the padded paws and noiseless step, the green eyes set in jet black fur with their grave regard, seemed to communicate calm and subdue agitation. Even Gosse's conversation would assume a more intimate and serene quality if it was accompanied by the purring of Caruso … In his essay on cats, Gosse … relates the story of 'Mahomet who, on being consulted one day on a point of piety, preferred to cut off his sleeve on which his favourite

pussy was asleep, rather than wake her violently by rising.'
Modern sartorial conditions would frustrate any such opera-
tion, but it was a gesture with which Gosse would have sym-
pathised. He would deprecate interruptions which involved
readjustment in his cat's scheme of inertia ... Théophile
Gautier divided his affection between cats and the singular
choice of white rats; Gosse favoured no other species of domestic animal, but like Chateaubriand and Victor Hugo, like
Baudelaire and Sainte-Beuve, gave his undivided preference
to cats.

Evan Charteris *Life and Letters of Sir Edmund Gosse*

My great-grandfather had, as I said, some skill in painting. He was gifted with an intense sense of, and love for, colour. I am sure he saw colours where other people did not. What to common eyes was a mass of grey, or green, was to him a pleasant combination of many gay and delicate hues. He distinguished severally the innumerable bright threads in nature's coat of many colours, and in simple truth I think that each was a separate joy to him.

He had a white Persian cat of an artistic temperament, which followed him on his walks, dozed on the back of his armchair, and condescended to share his tea when it reached a certain moderate temperature. It never was betrayed into excitement, except when there was fish for dinner. My great-grandfather's fasts were feasts for Thomas, the cat.

I can very clearly remember the sight of my great-grandfather pacing slowly up and down the tiny garden at The Vine, his hands behind him, and followed sedately by Thomas. Now and then he would stop to gaze, with infinite contentment in his eyes, at the delicate blue-grey mist behind the leafless trees (which in that spring sunshine were, no doubt, of much more complex and beautiful colour to him than mere brown), or drinking in the blue of the scillas in the border with a sigh of satisfaction. When he paused, Thomas would pause; as he feasted his eyes, Thomas would rub his head against his master's legs, and stretch his own. When Elspeth had cooked the fish, and my great-grandmother had made the tea and arranged the flowers on the table, they would come in together and condescend to their breakfasts, with the same air about them both of having no responsibility in life but to find out sunny spots, and to enjoy themselves.

Juliana Horatia Ewing from *Six to Sixteen* 1875

For every house is incompleat without him & a blessing
     is lacking in the spirit.

For the Lord commanded Moses concerning the cats at
     the departure of the Children of Israel from Egypt.

For every family had one cat at least in the bag.

For the English cats are the best in Europe.

For he is the cleanest in the use of his fore-paws of any
     quadruped.

For the dexterity of his defence is an instance of the love
     of God to him exceedingly.

For he is quickest to his mark of any creature.

For he is tenacious of his point.

For he is a mixture of gravity and waggery.

For he knows that God is his saviour.

For there is nothing sweeter than his peace when at rest.

For there is nothing brisker than his life when in motion.

Christopher Smart from *Rejoice in the Lamb, A Song from Bedlam*

ACKNOWLEDGEMENTS

Yvonne Skargon wishes warmly to thank Griselda Lewis and John
Commander for suggestions, help and encouragement in putting
together this small homage to a race of creatures to whom all three
are ridiculously in thrall.

The publishers gratefully acknowledge permission granted to
publish copyright material in this book by:

Anthony Powell for the entry from his *Journals* 1982-86,
Heinemann, 1995.

Enitharmon Press for three poems from Ruth Pitter's *Collected
Poems*, 1996.

Extract from *The Journal of Beatrix Potter 1881-1897*. Copyright
© Frederick Warne & Co., 1966, 1989. Reproduced by kind
permission of Frederick Warne & Co.

Everyman, J. M. Dent for Laurence Lerner's translation of *Cats* from Baudelaire, 1999.

James Michie for *Belling the Cat* from *Aesop's Fables*, Jonathan Cape, 1989.

Jennie by Paul Gallico, Copyright ©1950 Paul Gallico.

Martin Secker & Warburg for the passage from Colette's *My Mother's House*, trs. Una Vincenzo Troubridge and Enid McLeod, 1953.

Ronald Blythe for the passage from *Word from Wormingford*, Penguin Books, 1997.

Sinclair Stevenson for extracts from *The David Garnett and Sylvia Townsend Warner Letters,* edited by David Garnett, 1994.